Castles and Cannons

There are lots of Early Reader
stories you might enjoy.

Look at the back of the book,
or for a complete list, visit
www.orionchildrensbooks.co.uk

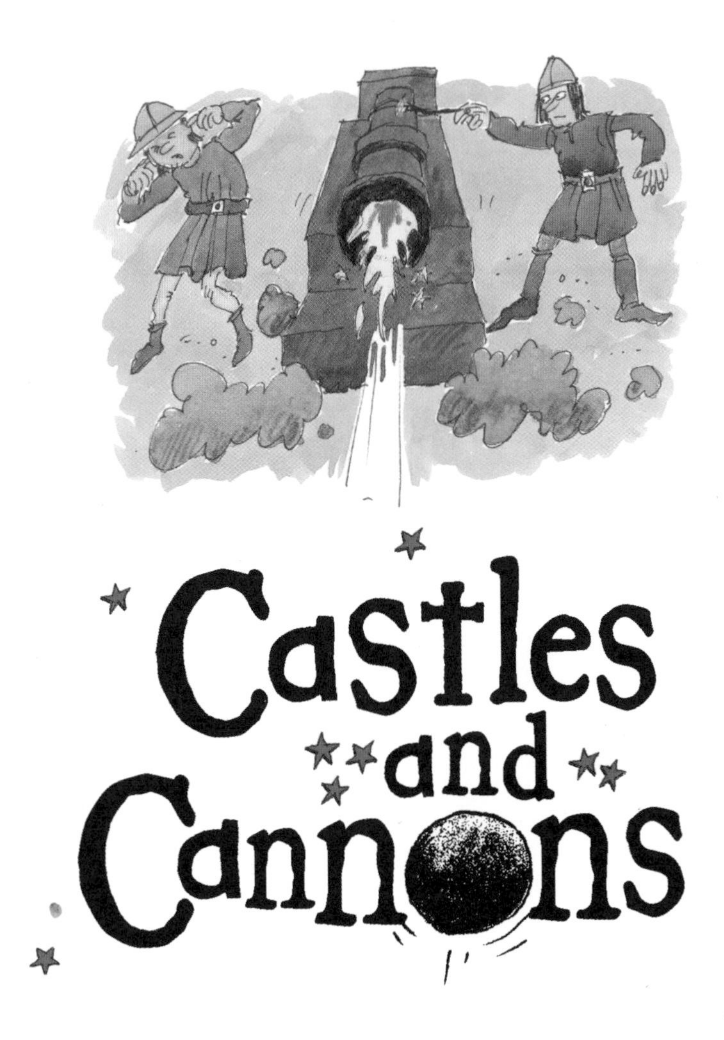

Castles and Cannons

Scoular Anderson

Orion
Children's Books

ORION CHILDREN'S BOOKS

First published in Great Britain in 2017
by Hodder and Stoughton

3 5 7 9 10 8 6 4 2

A CIP catalogue record for this book
is available from the British Library.

ISBN 978 1 4440 1564 5

Printed and bound in China

The paper and board used in this book are from well-managed
forests and other responsible sources.

Orion Children's Books
An imprint of
Hachette Children's Group
Part of Hodder and Stoughton
Carmelite House
50 Victoria Embankment
London EC4Y 0DZ

An Hachette UK Company
www.hachette.co.uk

www.hachettechildrens.co.uk

FOR KEAVA AND THOMAS ALEXANDER

CONTENTS

WHAT IS A CASTLE?

A long, long time ago, people were often in danger. Neighbours might come to take their land. There were attacks by wild animals. People needed a safe place to live.

A lord was a very important person. He lived in the very first kind of castle. It was called a motte and bailey castle.

motte

palisade

The castle sat on a mound, called the motte. The yard in front of the castle was called the bailey.

Castles got bigger and bigger. They were built to look really strong so that enemies were put off trying to attack them.

The main building was called the keep.

Many castles had one, two or even three high walls around them. There were towers built into the walls.

A big castle showed how important and powerful the lord was.

LIFE IN A CASTLE

People who lived in castles had titles like king, queen, baron, knight and lord and lady.

The lord and lady had private rooms where they got some peace away from the noise in the castle. They were quite comfortable.

Servants brought hot water for baths.

The loo was called a garderobe but it was just a hole in the wall...

...so it was a bit smelly outside!

Feasts were held in the great hall. This was the biggest room in the castle. The lord and lady and their important guests ate at a table up on a platform.

Acrobats and musicians performed during feasts. At night, many people slept here on the rushes which covered the floor.

The children of a lord and lady were looked after by servants. Children didn't go to school so they had plenty of time to play.

Older children were sent away to another castle. They had to serve the lord and lady there and learn good manners.

When a boy was a teenager he became a knight's servant called a squire. Knights were soldiers who fought on horseback.

A castle was a very busy place. There were hundreds of servants to look after the lord and lady.

Some were very important, like the chamberlain who looked after the lord's clothes and valuables. The steward was in charge of food. The constable looked after the guards and security.

Horses were very important for travel and in battle. There were grooms to look after them in the castle stables.

OUTSIDE THE CASTLE

Sometimes the lord called knights to his castle for a joust. This was an entertainment held outside the castle walls.

At the joust the knights showed off their fighting skills. Teams of knights charged at each other with lances.

It was a very colourful event with flags and tents and the knights dressed in bright clothes. People came from all around to cheer their favourite team.

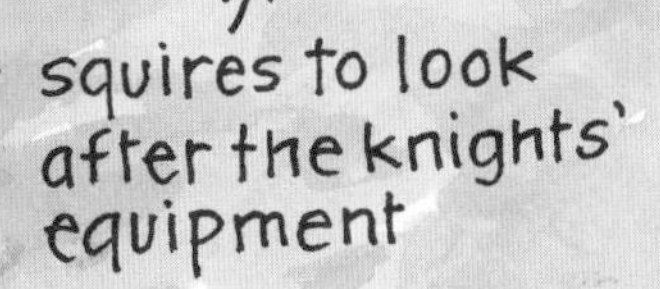

Hunting was the favourite sport of nobles. The lord kept a team of huntsmen in his castle to help with the hunt. Deer and boar were hunted with hounds. Smaller animals were hunted with hawks.

The lord and his guests sometimes hunted all day. Food was brought into the woods so the hunters could rest with a picnic.

After a joust or a hunt the castle marshall made sure the horses, dogs and falcons were well cared for.

BUILD BIG AND STRONG

Enemies attacked castle doors first because that was the weakest part on the walls. A castle usually had several things to protect the doors.

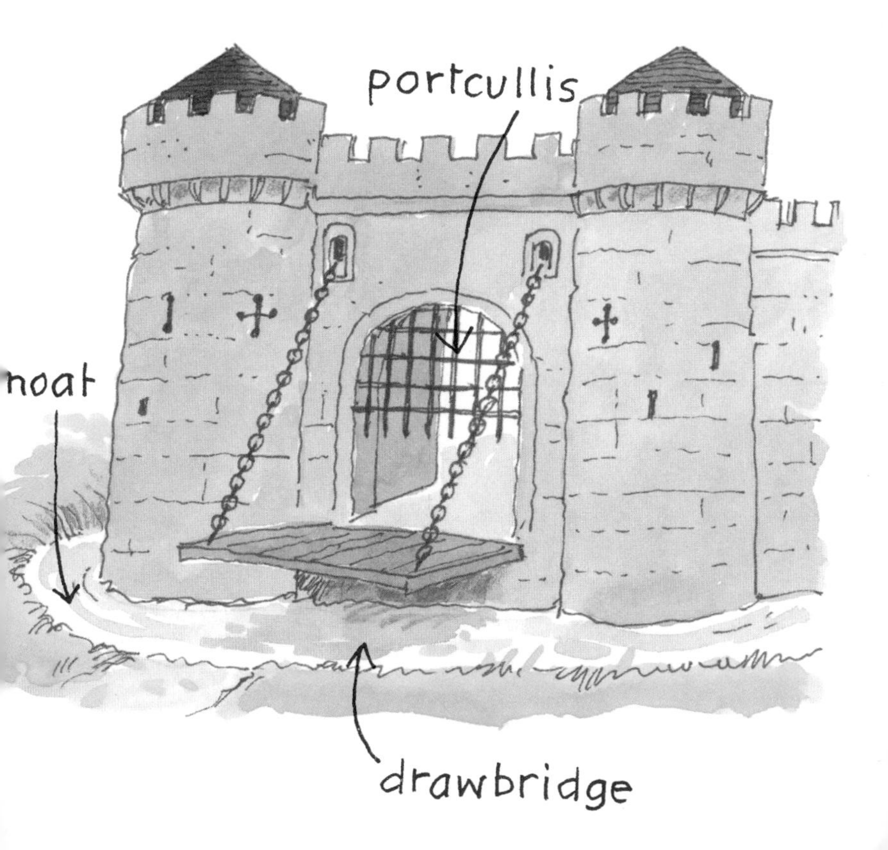

Castle walls were very thick and soldiers could stand on them. This area was called the battlements. The top of the walls had gaps so that weapons could be fired through them.

Soldiers also fired arrows through arrow loops in the castle walls. From the outside, the arrow loops looked like narrow windows.

Inside, there was room to fire arrows at any angle.

There were holes in the floor of the tower battlements. Arrows were fired through these or rocks were dropped on the enemy.

There were holes in the ceiling above the castle doors. If the enemy got through the doors things were dropped on them from above. The holes were known as murder holes.

Even though a castle looked strong, enemies still came to attack.

ATTACK!

When an enemy army reached a castle they surrounded it. No one could get in or out. This was called a siege. A siege lasted weeks – or even months.

The enemy attacked the castle door first. They used a battering ram. This was a huge tree trunk hung on ropes. It was swung back and forwards to smash down the door.

The battering ram was covered to protect the men using it. Soldiers on the battlements tried to stop them.

Next, the enemy tried to get over the battlements. They climbed the walls using ladders. This was very dangerous.

A wooden siege tower protected the attackers. The tower was covered in wet animal skins to stop the soldiers in the castle setting it on fire.

Sometimes, the enemy brought a giant catapult. It was called a trebuchet. It fired big stones at the castle walls.

A heavy weight hung from one end of a long pole. When the weight dropped, the pole swung round with great speed and flung a stone towards the castle.

Once there was a hole in the castle walls, the enemy could rush in.

TIME FOR A CHANGE

When a new weapon called a cannon was invented, people stopped building castles. A cannon could smash down thick walls very quickly. There was no point in building a castle.

The country became more peaceful so lords built big houses instead of castles. The biggest houses were called palaces. Kings and queens lived in palaces.

The big houses had hundreds of rooms and many large windows.

Sometimes, they had a very long room called a gallery. There was fine furniture here and paintings on the walls. People came to the gallery to meet, talk and walk.

The king and queen's bedroom had a huge bed called a four-poster. There were curtains round it to keep out the cold.

If the king and queen wanted to relax they sat in their drawing room. They read and played cards or a musical instrument.

At meal times, the king or lord ate with his family in a private dining room. When there were important guests for dinner, it took place in a large hall.

DINNER IS SERVED!

The palace kitchen was a busy place when a banquet was prepared for hundreds of guests.

A trumpeter sounded a fanfare when it was time to eat. The guests sat down at the tables. Musicians played while people ate.

The food arrived – all sorts of meat, fish, pies, tarts, salads, cheesecakes and vegetables with spices. For pudding there was a ship made out of pastry and sugar!

The candles glittered in the great hall of the palace. The gold stars painted on the ceiling twinkled. There was loud chatter and laughter.

A servant stood beside each guest to serve him or her with food and drink. Perhaps the guests were eating with the latest invention – a fork!

After dinner the guests joined in a masque. This was like a musical.

Everyone dressed in fancy costumes – even the king and queen. There was singing and dancing into the night.

The Tower of London

Caernarfon Castle, Wales

Stirling Castle, Scotland

Bamburgh Castle, Northumberland

Dover Castle, Kent